So Easy Publishing

Banbury, Oxfordshire, UK

So Easy Publishing is a trading name of ICT So Easy Ltd.

© So Easy Publishing and ICT So Easy Ltd, 2020

The moral rights of all author(s) have been asserted.

First published in 2020.

Acknowledgements

The author would like to thank his family for all their support both during the development of this book and throughout his educational career.

Cover image from Shutterstock. Other images are copyright free and sourced from www.goodfreephotos.com.

External links and references: *none identified*

Links to third party websites are provided in good faith and for information only. So Easy Publishing disclaims any responsibility for the materials contained in any third-party website reference in this work.

Getting Started with Arduino Projects

Learning Computing One Bit at a Time

Book Two

Contents

All examples and challenge solutions can be accessed online at the website https://ictsoeasy.co.uk/book2/

Introduction

Within the lifetime of the Author, the term 'Internet' has gone from one which literally didn't exist, akin to Science Fiction, to something which is so ubiquitous that we simply cannot imagine life without it.

When the precursor to the Internet, ARPANet, was developed in the 1960s, computers took up entire rooms – even entire buildings. The idea that one could walk around with such a device in one's pocket was little more than a dream.

Combining the concept of small yet powerful computers and the inter-connectivity afforded by the Internet gave rise to the Internet of Things (IoT), an idea rooted in a Coca-Cola machine in 1982 which reported its stock and temperature, but which wasn't coined as a term until 1999.

In this book we are not going to study IoT devices specifically. What we are going to do is look at how to develop some of the basic devices used within the IoT – specifically using the Arduino MicroController – and how we can add circuitry and programming to develop something which could be the start of a great little IoT device.

To illustrate the learning from this course we will use the Arduino microcontroller. While we love playing with physical hardware, the examples and tutorials will be based around the emulator, Tinkercad, available online at https://www.tinkercad.com/ – you will need to create an account (or sign in with a Google account). Should you wish to follow along with physical hardware a short guide is available at the end of this book.

TinkerCad provides an *emulator* – it acts like the Arduino hardware and software but runs within a website.

1: Getting Started with TinkerCad

Before we can do much we need to get on to the software. Like so many modern websites TinkerCad allows you to use a Google account so we recommend you sign up for by going to https://accounts.google.com/ and clicking on "Create account".

Once that is done, follow these steps;

1. Go to https://www.tinkercad.com/
2. Click on "JOIN NOW" in the top right hand corner.
3. Click on "Create a personal account".
4. Click on "Sign in with Google" and enter your Google 9account details.
5. Once you are in, click on "Circuits" on the left hand side.
6. Finally, click "Create new Circuit" to open up a blank workspace for us to build our circuit on.

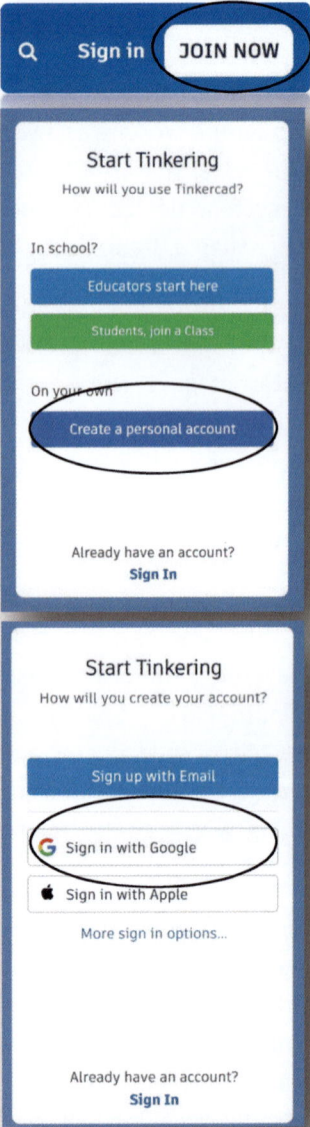

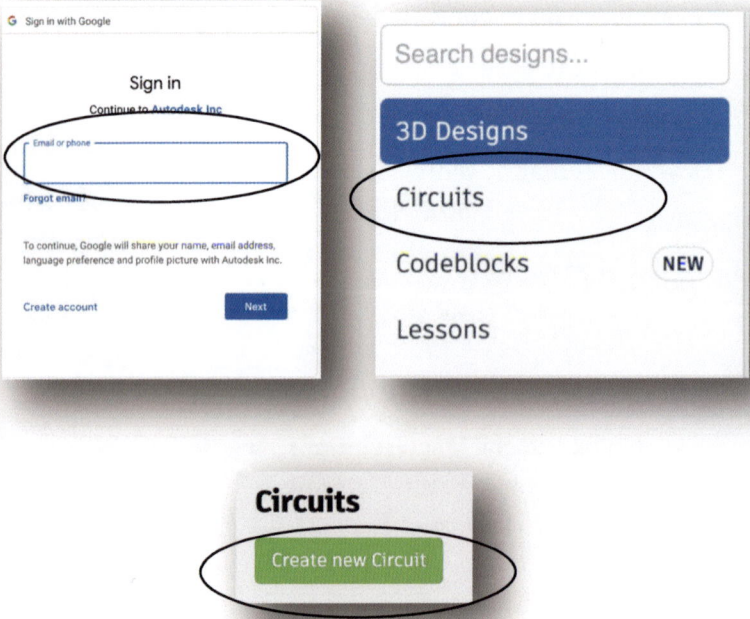

Building Our First Circuit

We build a device with three things:

1. A **microcontroller** (the Arduino) which follows instructions and interacts with other hardware.
2. A **circuit** consisting of hardware (components) joined together with wires.
3. Software, programming code that tells the microcontroller how to react in a given situation.

In this section we are going to build our hardware by creating a circuit and connecting it to our Arduino. We can add components, including the Arduino, on to our workspace by searching for it and then dragging it on to the workspace.

Go ahead and also add a breadboard (the mini one will do), an LED and a resistor.

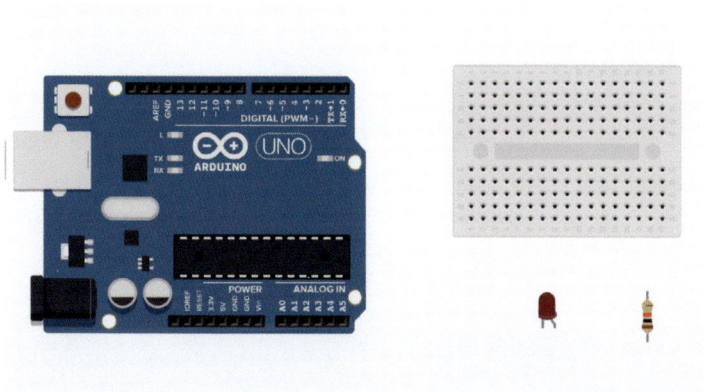

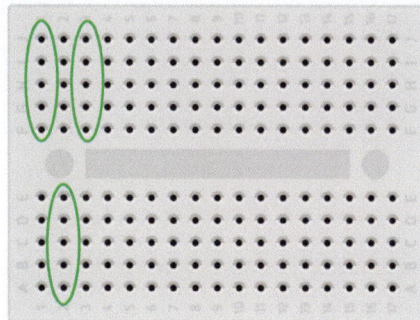

These images show us searching for components.

The breadboard is a handy tool used for developing circuits. Each column of five holes is connected, so you can plug components in and they become joined without needing to use wires or soldering them. The picture below shows how the holes are joined (each green shape being holes that are connected).

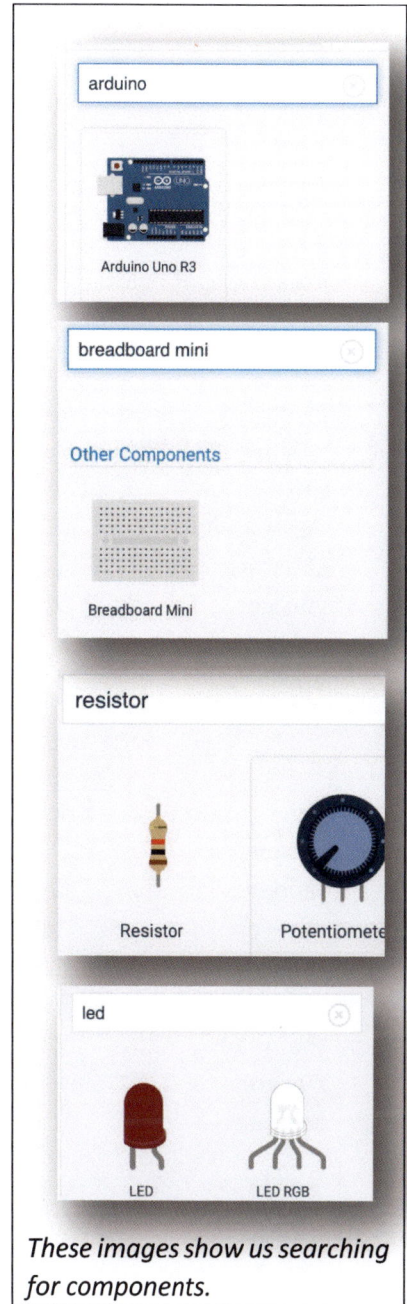

We can drag and drop the components on to the breadboard. Go ahead and put the LED and the resistor on the breadboard like the picture below.

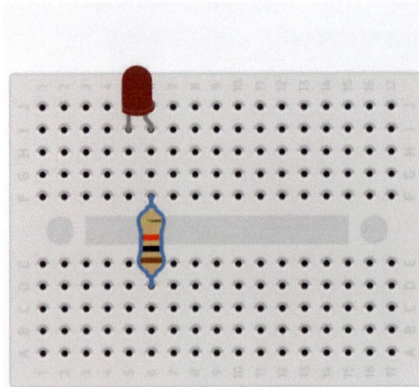

The top leg of the resistor and the right leg of the LED are connected because they are on the same column. The top and bottom legs of the resistor are *not* joined because of the central gap.

Now we can start wiring things up! You simply click where you want one end of the wire to go, and then click where you want the other end to go. You can double click anywhere in the middle of the wire to make a bend.

I've connected the *left* leg of the LED (called the *cathode*) to one of the GND sockets on the Arduino and the bottom leg of the LED to the 5V socket on the Arduino. I've also changed the colours so that red is the positive wire and black the ground wire, so I can see what I'm doing a bit better.

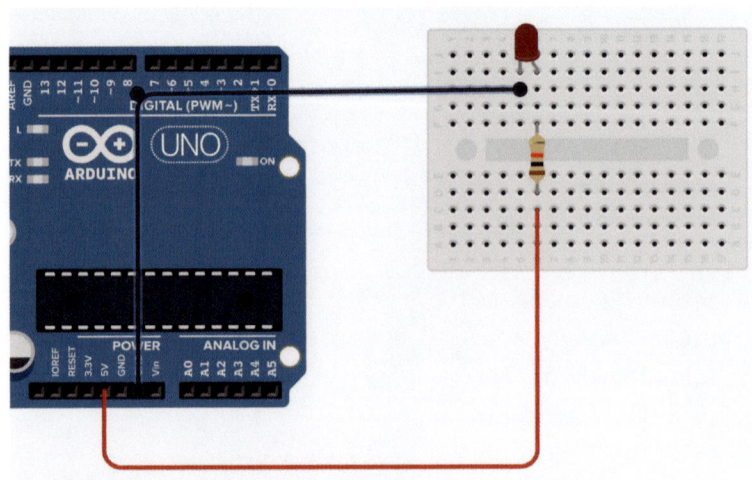

If you click the **Start Simulation** button you will see your LED light up (yay).

LED stands for Light Emitting Diode – they are like little light bulbs.

Electricity flows from positive (in this example the 5 volt socket) to negative (ground or GND). LEDs are directional so if you get it the wrong way around they won't light up!

Too much electricity getting to LEDs has a tendency to make them set on fire. Resistors reduce the amount getting through – you can click on them and change them. I've gone for 220 Ohms for this one.

What we've done so far is just using the Arduino as a battery. Those other pins let us do a bit more – we want to be able to turn our LED on and off at will. Grab the end of the red wire and drag it up to pin 8. This is a digital pin, nice and easy to turn on and off.

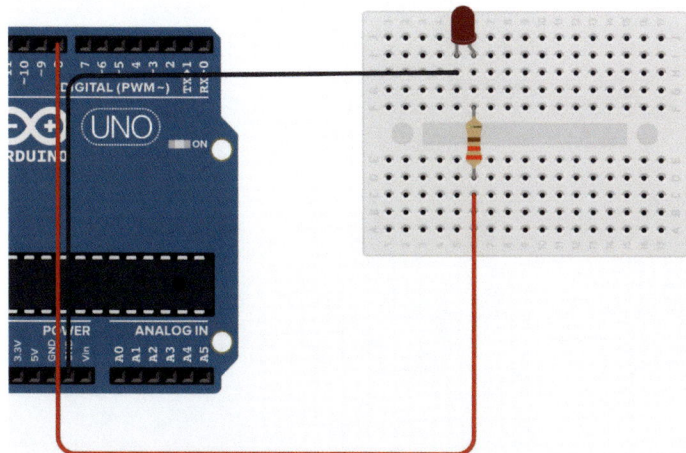

You can program TinkerCad a bit like Scratch, with blocks of code. But using text is a bit more fun and certainly more powerful!

If you click **Start Simulation** again you will notice it no longer turns on. That's because we haven't told it to! Press the **Code** button and then select **Blocks**.

You may have noticed that when you started your simulation earlier, a little light on the Arduino was blinking. This is the built in LED, and the code is already written to make it blink. Let's just adapt this code to work for our LED!

The **setup** routine at the top tells the Arduino that pin number 13 is going to be used for **output**. We are using pin 8 instead of the (built in) pin 13, so change 13 to 8 in there.

Output is when a machine such as the Arduino sends out a signal of some kind. When it receives a signal (such as you pressing a button) it is called **input**.

The **loop** routine just runs over and over again, it tells pin 13 (the built in LED) to go **high** – that is to have a high voltage (which makes the LED light up), to wait 1,000 milliseconds (1 second), go **low** (low voltage, turn off), wait 1,000 milliseconds again, then repeat. That's all fine but we are using pin 8, not pin 13, so go ahead and change those 13s to 8s, then hit **Start Simulation** again – watch that LED blink!

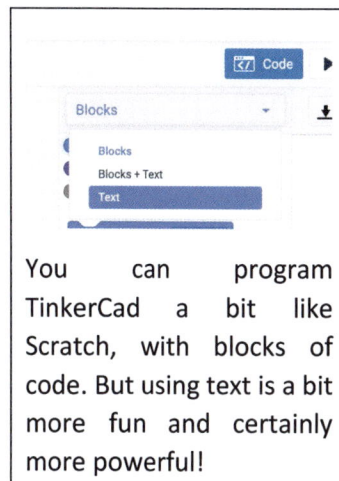

If you struggle to follow the descriptions you can always go look at our example at:

ictsoeasy.co.uk/book2/#B2Ex1

Your code should now look like this:

```
void setup()
{
    pinMode(8, OUTPUT);
}


void loop()
{
    digitalWrite(8, HIGH);
    delay(1000); // Wait for 1000 millisecond(s)
    digitalWrite(8, LOW);
    delay(1000); // Wait for 1000 millisecond(s)
}
```

The orange bits starting with // are comments – the computer will just ignore them. The important things to remember are:

- **pinMode** tells the Arduino whether the pin is input or output.
- **digitalWrite** tells a pin to write a high or low value.
- **delay** waits a number of (milliseconds).

Challenges
Why not try the following:

1. Make the LED flash on and off quickly, then slowly.
2. Add a second LED that flashes at a different time.

You can see our answers to the challenges here:

ictsoeasy.co.uk/book2/#B2Ch1
and...
ictsoeasy.co.uk/book2/#B2Ch1

2: Responding to a button

So far we have learnt how to have our Arduino turn an LED on and off when *it* thinks it is the right time, but for a device to be a bit more useful we want to be able to respond to outside stimulus – we want to be able to *turn the light on*.

Setting up the Breadboard

So far we have used our breadboard just to hold on to some components and connect them together. But when things get a bit more complex (like having lots of things needing positive and ground connections) we can get a bit more clever. If you replace your mini breadboard with a small breadboard like the one shown here, you will see a black and a red bar running across the top and bottom of the board. These are *power rails* – we connect the ground and 5V connections to these from the Arduino and can then connect to power much easier. From now on, our starting circuit will look like this:

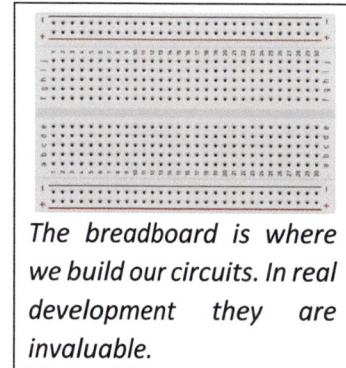

The breadboard is where we build our circuits. In real development they are invaluable.

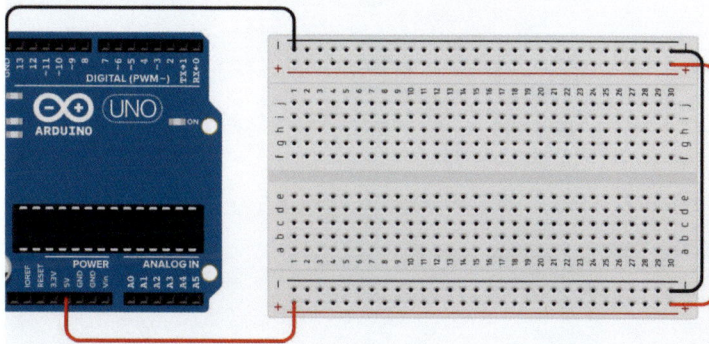

This lets us pick up power and ground very easily when we need to. You can access, and use, this as a starting point for your projects here: ictsoeasy.co.uk/book2/#B2Ex2

Adding a Button

Before we start building our circuit it's a good idea to get your components together. Search for and drag on to your workspace an LED, a pushbutton, and two resistors.

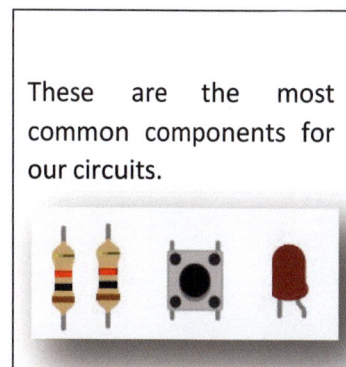

These are the most common components for our circuits.

The button is separated left from right so any electricity flowing into one of the left hand legs cannot get through until you press the button, at which point the electricity can flow through to the right hand leg and complete the circuit.

We could, therefore, just use the Arduino as a battery again and just put the pushbutton before the LED in the circuit, like this.

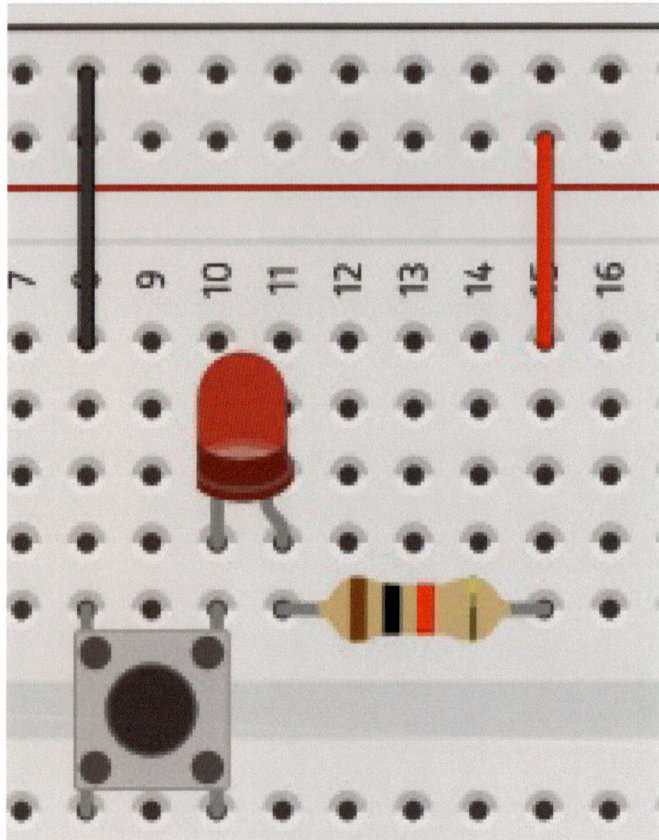

Why not build this circuit or access ours at:

ictsoeasy.co.uk/book2/#B2Ex3

Start the simulation and try the button out.

In this example the electricity flows from the positive (red) rail through the red wire into one end of the resistor (which I have set to 220 Ohms), through the resistor, into the LED and then into one leg of the switch, where it stops. As the circuit is incomplete the LED does not light up. If I push the switch, the electricity can complete it's circuit by running through the black wire to the ground rail. The circuit is complete and the LED lights up.

However this again is defeating the object of having a microcontroller. We want the Arduino to *detect* a button has been pressed and then *decide* to light up the LED. For this we need to build a slightly different circuit, like the one below.

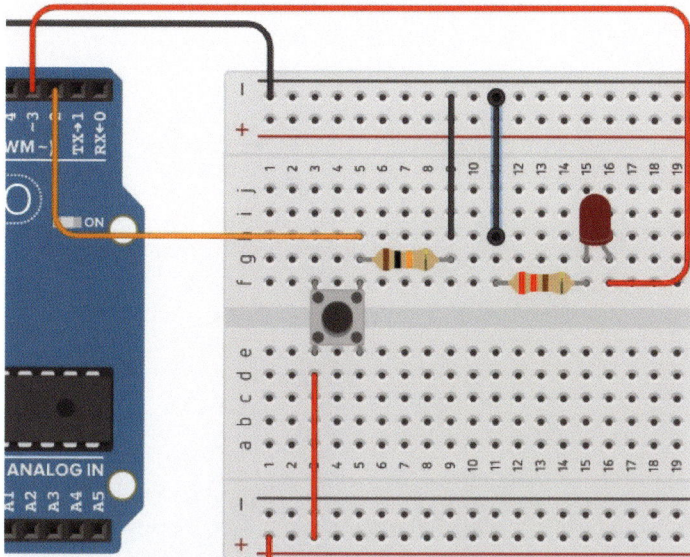

This is called a PULL DOWN resistor circuit because the electricity is pulled down to ground. If you don't do this the circuit *may* still work but as the voltage is 'floating' it can get a bit confused. In real circuits this can cause all sorts of odd problems!

Wow things are getting a bit confused, aren't they? Don't worry, there's nothing too scary happening. We actually have two circuits here;

1. When pin 3 is set HIGH, the electricity flows out of pin 3 down the red wire, into the LED, through the 220 Ohm resistor to stop it getting too much power, and back to ground on the top rail.

2. Electricity flows from the (bottom) positive rail in to the left hand side of the switch, and stops as the switch is open. Pin 2 is reading whether or not there is any electricity coming through the orange wire, and as the only route it has is through the resistor (which I set to 10 kOhms) to ground, it detects no (LOW) voltage. When we push the button, however, that electricity from the red wire can flow through the switch. Getting through a 10 kOhms resistor to ground is quite hard, however, so it flows through the orange wire into pin 2, giving a HIGH reading.

k stands for kilo – a thousand. A kilo-Ohm or kOhm is 1,000 Ohms.

Programming a Button Response

Of course our circuit won't do anything unless we program the Arduino to detect the button press and turn on/off the LED. If we go in to the code button and choose **text** again, we can enter this code:

```
void setup()

{

  pinMode(2, INPUT);

  pinMode(3, OUTPUT);

}


void loop()

{

  if (digitalRead(2) == HIGH) {

    digitalWrite(3, HIGH);

  } else {

    digitalWrite(3, LOW);

  }

}
```

So what are we doing here? First of all we are telling the Arduino about the pins we are using. We are using pin 3 as an OUTPUT pin like previously, but now we have pin 2 as an INPUT pin as well.

Then we are going to go around in the loop. We read what pin 2 is saying. If it is HIGH then the button has been pressed and is letting the electricity through. THEN we tell pin 3 to be HIGH (turn the LED on). Otherwise (else) we tell pin 3 to be LOW (off). Then we go around the loop again! You can see our working example here: ictsoeasy.co.uk/book2/#B2Ex4

setup() and **loop()** are subroutines which are added to every Arduino program automatically. **setup()** is called at the start of the program and **loop()** is then called over and over again.

== is called an *equality operator* – it means "are the two sides the same?"

Challenges

Why not try the following?

3. Make the LED turn OFF when the button is pressed and ON when it is not.
4. Extend challenge 3 to have one LED turn ON and another OFF when the button is pressed, and the opposite when it is not pressed.

You can see our answers to the challenges here:

ictsoeasy.co.uk/book2/#B2Ch3 and...
ictsoeasy.co.uk/book2/#B2Ch4

3: Latching Buttons using Variables

You have probably noticed that as soon as you leave go, the LED turns off. That's somewhat annoying isn't it? If only we had some way to *remember* that the button was pressed. Oh – we do! We call a bit of memory a variable.

We will use the same circuit as the last one we created but change the code. Replace the existing code with this:

```
boolean LEDOn = true;
```

A Boolean is a variable that can be either true or false. This idea is right at the heart of Computer Science! We *initialised* this variable to have the value 'true'.

```
void setup()
{
  pinMode(2, INPUT);
  pinMode(3, OUTPUT);
}


void loop()
{
  if (digitalRead(2) == HIGH) {
    LEDOn = not LEDOn;
  }
```

The *not* command *inverts* a Boolean variable – if it's true it becomes false, it it's false it becomes true.

```
  if (LEDOn == true) {
    digitalWrite(3, HIGH);
  } else {
    digitalWrite(3, LOW);
  }
}
```

Now we can test what the variable is and either set the LED on, or the LED off.

Try the program and see what happens! Our example is available here: ictsoeasy.co.uk/book2/#B2Ex5

Do it Better!

When you run the program you should be able to *toggle* the LED on and off by pressing the button. Hurrah! But *sometimes* you may notice it doesn't quite work out. This is because the microprocessor is *really* quick and sometimes it detects you've pressed the button once, then goes and detects it again before you have had time to take your finger off!

Change your code to this:

We set another Boolean to identify whether we need to keep checking or not.

```
boolean LEDOn = true;
boolean stopChecking = false;

void setup()
{
  pinMode(2, INPUT);
  pinMode(3, OUTPUT);
}
```

We only set that we can keep checking if they button is *not* pressed.

We *nest* another check outside the code we wrote before. If we've said to stop checking, we don't do any of this. When we invert the LEDOn variable we set 'stopChecking' so that we don't do it again until the button is let up.

```
void loop()
{
  if (digitalRead(2) == LOW) {
    stopChecking = false;
  }

  if (stopChecking == false) {
    if (digitalRead(2) == HIGH) {
      stopChecking = true;
      LEDOn = not LEDOn;
    }

    if (LEDOn == true) {
        digitalWrite(3, HIGH);
    } else {
        digitalWrite(3, LOW);
    }
  }
  delay(50);
}
```

We added a little delay just in case the button bounces a bit as we press it.

Again, our version is here: ictsoeasy.co.uk/book2/#B2Ex6

Challenges

5. Can you adapt this code so that when you latch one LED on, a second one latches off, and vice versa?
6. Can you add a second button so that one button turns the LED on, and the second turns the LED off?

You can see our answers to the challenges here:

ictsoeasy.co.uk/book2/#B2Ch5
and...
ictsoeasy.co.uk/book2/#B2Ch6

4: Analogue Input & Output

Serial Monitor

One of the biggest differences between programming a microcontroller such as an Arduino, and programming on a computer using something such as Python, is that it can be really difficult to see what's going on without a monitor! One thing we can do is make use of the serial monitor which allows the Arduino to send text to the computer it's connected to (even virtually like in TinkerCad) so we can look at values.

Go back to our basic circuit with just the breadboard and Arduino. Go to code and type in this:

```
void setup()
{
  Serial.begin(9600);
}

void loop()
{
  Serial.print("Hello ");
  Serial.println("World");
  delay(250);
}
```

Open the Serial Monitor (at the bottom right of the screen) and click **Start Simulation.**

You have to start serial communication in the setup, else the Arduino won't know to open up the channel. The 9600 is the speed (baud rate) – we can just leave it as it is here.

Serial.print() sends a bit of text to the monitor. Note that unlike some programming, you *have* to use double quotes.

Serial.println() does the same – but then sends a new line (like pressing return on your keyboard).

The delay is just so you can see what is happening.

> Serial communication is where a single piece of data is sent at a time. It's simple and works well. Arduinos can send a single character at a time.

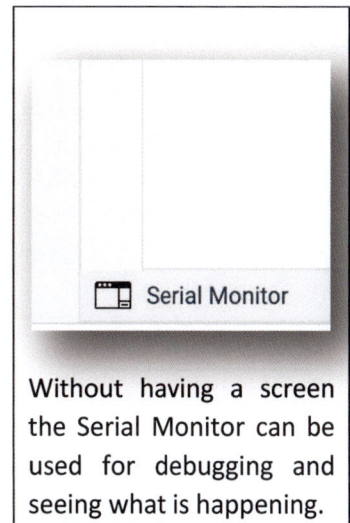

Serial Monitor

> Without having a screen the Serial Monitor can be used for debugging and seeing what is happening.

> If you struggle to follow the descriptions you can always go look at our example at:
>
> ictsoeasy.co.uk/book2/#B2Ex7

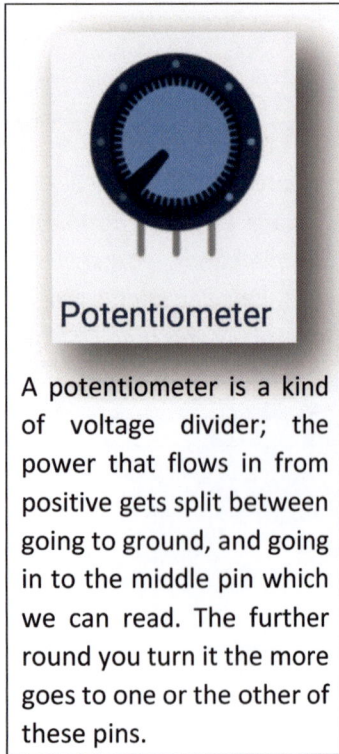

Potentiometer

A potentiometer is a kind of voltage divider; the power that flows in from positive gets split between going to ground, and going in to the middle pin which we can read. The further round you turn it the more goes to one or the other of these pins.

Note the spelling – analog is the American spelling of analogue. Computers normally use American spellings.

An *integer* is a whole number.

Reading an Analogue Device

Let's go back and in a potentiometer.

We now need to connect it up so that the left leg is connected to ground, the right leg is connected to positive, and the middle leg is connected to an *analogue* input pin – we have chosen A0 in our example at ictsoeasy.co.uk/book2/#B2Ex8

Now go to code and type in this code:

```
int sensorValue;

void setup()
{
   Serial.begin(9600);
}

void loop()
{
   sensorValue = analogRead(A0);
   Serial.println(sensorValue);
   delay(250);
}
```

We created an *integer* variable and used analogRead() instead of digitalRead() to get the position of the sensor. Note that the lowest you can go is 0 (nothing obviously) but the highest is 1023 which is the biggest number an Arduino can read – it has 1024 possible values.

Outputting in Analogue

So first of all we need to know a bit more about what the difference is between analogue and digital. Most real world data is analogue – it is *continuous*. When the temperature changes from 30C to 31C it doesn't jump, it has to go through all the variations between the two on its way.

Digital data is *discrete* – when counting the number of pigeons in a row we count 1… 2… we don't have to go through 'bits' of pigeons between them.

Computers cannot store analogue data because there is *infinite* variations between two points of analogue data. So it has to sample them and restrict the variations it measures. So even though we could turn the potentiometer a tiny teenie bit the Arduino has to decide which of it's 1024 numbers is closest, converting it into digital data. This is why we have to use analogue pins, because the digital pins don't know how to do that!

As well as reading analogue data, we can output an approximation of analogue data using something called PWM (don't worry about what that means – just know that on the Arduino it has a ~ next to the pin number!)

We can use this to do some clever things – for example by outputting a bit *less* voltage we can make an LED dimmer.

> Although analogue can be read between 0 and 1023, PWM can only write between 0 and 255. PWM is a way of using digital output to *simulate* analogue.

First of all, create a simple LED circuit like you did earlier:

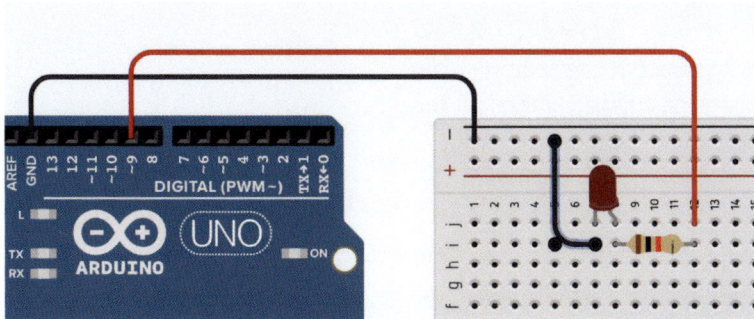

We have used pin 9, notice it has the ~ to indicate it is PWM?

Now enter this code:

```
int brightness = 0;

void setup() {
  pinMode(9, OUTPUT);
}

void loop() {
  analogWrite(9, brightness);
  brightness = brightness + 5;

  if (brightness >= 255) {
    brightness = 0;
  }

  delay(30);
}
```

> This section tests if the brightness is more than, or equal to, 255 (the maximum value) and resets it if needed.

You can always have a look at our example here: ictsoeasy.co.uk/book2/#B2Ex9

Challenges:

You may notice the challenge are getting harder. That's ok, they're meant to be challenging and this book is only ever meant to be an introduction! You can always have a look at our worked examples.

7. Can you combine the lessons from this section so that you can turn the potentiometer to adjust the LED brightness. **Hint**: remember the potentiometer goes 0-1023 and the LED can only take 0-255? If we divide the potentiometer by 4 we get something close enough to use. Something like this...
   ```
   int newLED = potentiometerReading/4;
   ```
8. Can you extend challenge 7 to output the reading from the potentiometer, and the calculated value of the LED, to the serial monitor?

> You can see our answers to the challenges here:
>
> ictsoeasy.co.uk/book2/#B2Ch7
> and...
> ictsoeasy.co.uk/book2/#B2Ch8

5: Using Analogue to our Advantage

We've already looked at a potentiometer and how to read it using an analogue pin. The things we could do with one are boundless; One thing we could do is use the potentiometer to select one of a number of options by using it to scroll between LEDs.

Go back to your basic breadboard, then add on a potentiometer, 5 LEDs and 5 resistors (set them all to 220 Ohms).

The potentiometer is wired up as before, with the outside legs going to ground and positive and the middle one to A0 (the yellow wire). The LEDs have the left leg's (cathode) connected to ground, and the right legs (anode) going through a resistor to pins 3,4,5,6 & 7.

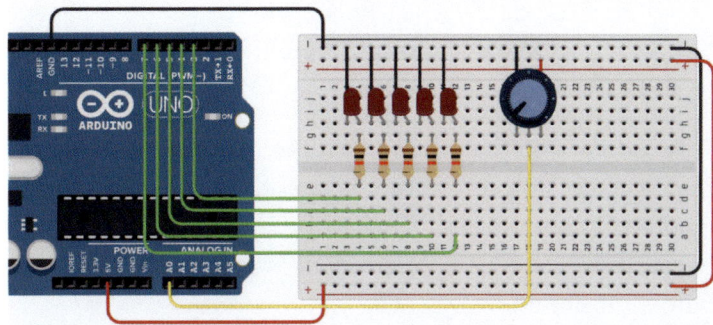

We want to be able to turn the potentiometer all the way left to light up the first LED, a *bit* left to turn on the second, mid-way to turn on the third, and so on.

The first thing to do is to check what readings we get with the potentiometer in these positions. Enter this code:

```
int potReading = 0;

void setup() {
  pinMode(A0, INPUT);
  Serial.begin(9600);
}

void loop() {
  potReading = analogRead(A0);
  Serial.println(potReading);
  delay(50);
}
```

You can see we've shortened 'potentiometer' to pot – this is a common short name

You can always have a look at our example here: ictsoeasy.co.uk/book2/#B2Ex10

Run the program and write down the numbers you see on the serial monitor with the potentiometer in five positions.

We got these results:

Potentiometer Position	Reading
Full Left	1023
Half Left	798
Middle	511
Half Right	246
Full Right	0

Although 0 and 1023 are fairly easy to hit, you may have got slightly different numbers for the middle three positions. This is as it is quite difficult to judge exact points on the potentiometer – and you will notice even bigger differences if you try this with real hardware. Therefore, we will use ranges to check that the potentiometer is roughly in the right place.

This code will do the logic to turn the LEDs on or off. Notice that we have just put a comment (a note for the programmer, ignored by the Arduino) in place of the running code? This is because we want to write codes in little bits and test them before moving on.

```
void loop() {
  potReading = analogRead(A0);
  Serial.println(potReading);
  if (potReading < 123) {
    //turn on LED 1
  } else {
    if (potReading < 379) {
      //turn on LED 2
    } else {
      if (potReading < 655) {
        //turn on LED 3
      } else {
        if (potReading < 911) {
          //turn on LED 4
        } else {
          //turn on LED 5
        }
      }
    }
  }
  delay(50);
}
```

We chose numbers about half way between our selected points . We used *nested* decisions – if the reading is less than 123, it must be LED 1. Otherwise (else) it can't be, so we put another check in to see if it's LED 2, and so on. We don't need to check LED 5, because if it's not 1, 2, 3 or 4 it *must* be LED 5!

You can always have a look at our example here: ictsoeasy.co.uk/book2/#B2Ex11

So how about turning the LEDs on? Actually that's fairly easy, we just send the relevant one the HIGH signal. But we will also have to send all the others a LOW signal, which means we are going to be repeating ourselves a lot.

What we can do is create a subroutine (like `loop` and `setup`) which we can call on to turn off *all* the LEDs and then we just have to turn *on* the one we want.

Our code is getting quite long so we had to split it across two columns! Just write the left column then carry on and write the right column underneath it.

You can always have a look at our example here: ictsoeasy.co.uk/book2/#B2Ex12

```
int potReading = 0;

void setup() {
  pinMode(A0, INPUT);
  pinMode(3, OUTPUT);
  pinMode(4, OUTPUT);
  pinMode(5, OUTPUT);
  pinMode(6, OUTPUT);
  pinMode(7, OUTPUT);
  Serial.begin(9600);
}

void turnAllOff() {
  digitalWrite(3,LOW);
  digitalWrite(4,LOW);
  digitalWrite(5,LOW);
  digitalWrite(6,LOW);
  digitalWrite(7,LOW);
}

void loop() {
  potReading = analogRead(A0);
  Serial.println(potReading);
  if (potReading < 123) {
    turnAllOff();
    //turn on LED 1
    digitalWrite(3,HIGH);
  } else {
    if (potReading < 379) {
        turnAllOff();
      //turn on LED 2
      digitalWrite(4,HIGH);
    } else {
      if (potReading < 655) {
        turnAllOff();
        //turn on LED 3
        digitalWrite(5,HIGH);
      } else {
        if (potReading < 911) {
          turnAllOff();
          //turn on LED 4
          digitalWrite(6,HIGH);
        } else {
          turnAllOff();
          //turn on LED 5
          digitalWrite(7,HIGH);
        }
      }
    }
  }
  delay(50);
}
```

Subroutines to Save Repetition

When we find ourselves doing identical things in different places, it is generally a good idea to create a subroutine to do the repeated steps. This is part of *pattern recognition.* But you will often find yourself doing *similar* things repeatedly. Here we are telling turning off all the LEDs, then lighting a new one up, but the new one varies.

We can actually build this in to our subroutine. Instead of just acting dumbly to turn off all the LEDs we can pass the routine some information (called a parameter). This parameter can be the number of the pin to turn *on.* So we could replace our `turnAllOff` routine with `turnOneOn` – as below:

```
void turnOneOn(int OnPin) {
   digitalWrite(3,LOW);
   digitalWrite(4,LOW);
   digitalWrite(5,LOW);
   digitalWrite(6,LOW);
   digitalWrite(7,LOW);
   digitalWrite(OnPin,HIGH);
}
```

The information inside the brackets on the first line tell it to expect a *parameter* that will be an integer, and we will call it OnPin. In the last line, we then use the parameter in place of the pin number to turn the LED on HIGH. Whatever number OnPin is set to will be used in the digitalWrite command.

We can then call the subroutine by including an integer parameter:

```
turnOneOn(4);
```

Will turn off all the LEDs and then turn *on* pin 4. This makes our code a lot easier to read, and much easier to write!

Challenges:
9. Can you add another 2 LEDs so that you can turn a *bit* left and a *lot* left (and the same right)?
10. Can you edit challenge 9 so that three LEDs light up (the ones either side of the one you choose)? Hint: parameters, like numbers, can have sums done on them using + and -).

You can see our answers to the challenges here:

ictsoeasy.co.uk/book2/#B2Ch9
and...
ictsoeasy.co.uk/book2/#B2Ch10

Photodiode

Ambient Light Sensor...

IR sensor

Ultrasonic Distance Sensor

SW 200Ω

Tilt Sensor

Tilt Sensor 4-pin

Gas Sensor

A sensor is any device which detects a physical property and passes a signal to be processed. There are many sensors available on the market, costing from pennies to a significant amount of money – choosing the right one can be tricky!

If you struggle to follow the descriptions you can always go look at our example at:

ictsoeasy.co.uk/book2/#B2Ex14

6: Making a Useful System

For the final project we thought it would be useful to look at combining what we've learnt so far into a useful system. How about building a system of lighting and temperature control?

One thing at a time, we've already learned how to use analogue sensors, so it's just a case of finding the right ones. We will add a Temperature Sensor and a Photoresistor and wire them up as below.

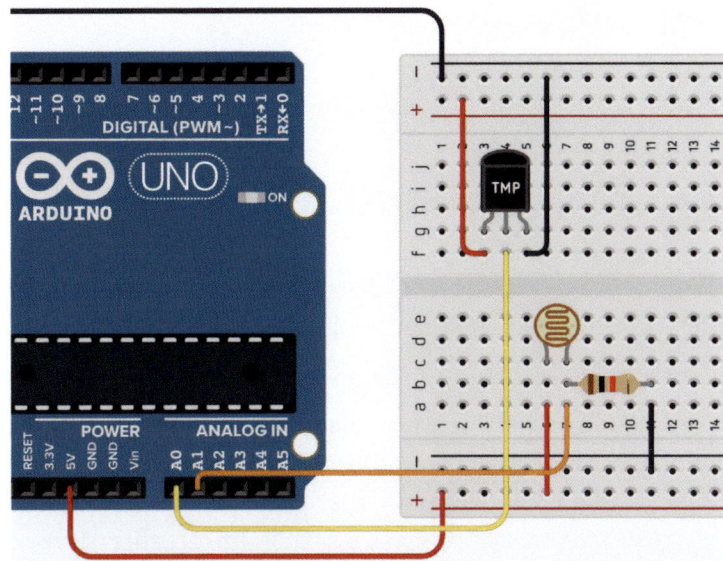

The temperature sensor is fairly simple, it's just like the potentiometer with one side being positive, one side being ground and the middle being the signal wire. The photoresistor is a bit more pickly though! We have to wire that up like a switch, with the resistor pulling the electricity down to ground and then the photoresistor just registering the different light conditions and passing along a signal. That resistor is a 10 kOhm by the way!

Now we can add some code to make sure we've got everything right. This is going to be just like when we read the potentiometer reading, only this time we will read both A0 and A1, and we will pass them back to the serial monitor every 250ms (every quarter of a second).

```
int tempReading = 0;
int lightReading = 0;

void setup() {
  pinMode(A0, INPUT);
  pinMode(A0, INPUT);
  Serial.begin(9600);
}

void loop() {
  tempReading = analogRead(A0);
  lightReading = analogRead(A1);
  Serial.print("Temp: ");
  Serial.println(tempReading);
  Serial.print("Light: ");
  Serial.println(lightReading);
  delay(250);
}
```

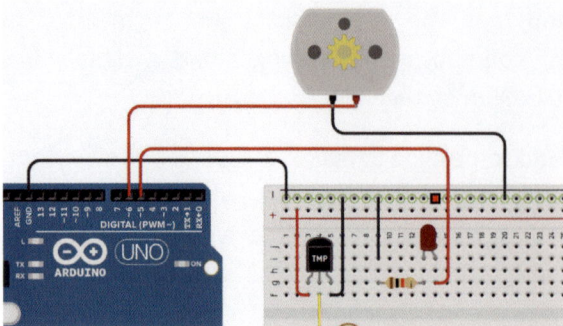

Both the sensors can be clicked so you can adjust the temperature and/or brightness.

We can use this to see what inputs from each correspond to the values we are sensing. We'll think about that in just a moment.

Let's have a think... as we're managing to control light and temperature, what *output* devices would make sense? Well, if it gets dark we turn a light on. That's simple! And if it's hot we can turn a fan on. We don't have a fan in TinkerCad, but we do have a DC motor, and if we have a DC motor we could do all *sorts* of things, make it turn on a tap, open the window, or even attach a fan to it!

So let's add on a DC motor, an LED, and a 220 Ohm resistor for the LED so it doesn't set on fire and set the smoke alarm off!

An input device sends data to a system to be processed (like a keyboard, or a sensor). An output device receives instruction *from* a system (like your monitor, speakers, or an LED we tell to turn on)

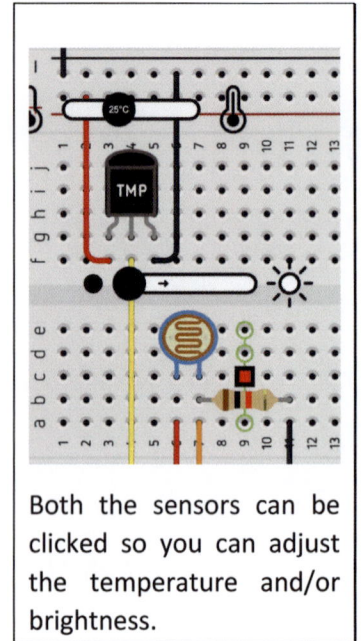

Note we have connected the LED through the resistor but the motor is directly to a pin from the Arduino? We'll discuss this shortly!

You will notice that we have chosen to turn the fan *on* at 155, but *off* at 151. If we just turned it on at 155 and off when the reading dropped below that we would find that as the temperature hovered around that setting, or as power fluctuated a little bit due to interference, the fan would be constantly stopping and starting. The exact measurements are often due to trial and error, however!

If you struggle to follow the descriptions you can always go look at our example at:

ictsoeasy.co.uk/book2/#B2Ex15

How slow is that DC motor?

```
int tempReading = 0;
int lightReading = 0;

void setup() {
  pinMode(A0, INPUT);
  pinMode(A0, INPUT);
  pinMode(5, OUTPUT);
  pinMode(6, OUTPUT);
  Serial.begin(9600);
}

void loop() {
  tempReading = analogRead(A0);
  lightReading = analogRead(A1);
  Serial.print("Temp: ");
  Serial.println(tempReading);
  if (tempReading > 155) {
    digitalWrite(6,HIGH);
  }
  if (tempReading < 151) {
    digitalWrite(6,LOW);
  }
  Serial.print("Light: ");
  Serial.println(lightReading);
  if (lightReading < 500) {
    digitalWrite(5,HIGH);
  }
  if (lightReading > 550) {
    digitalWrite(5,LOW);
  }
  delay(250);
}
```

There are two things we need be very aware of here, however. DC motors. DC motors have varying voltage requirements. Some are 5v which is what we're using from our Arduino. Yay. Some, however, are 9v and so won't spin as fast as they should, and some are lower (such as 3.3v) which will turn too fast and damage at least the motor, if not our Arduino! The other problem we have is, if you run your circuit, the motor is spinning *very* slowly (ours was spinning just 12 times a second!) This is because the Arduino pins put out very little actual power (current). What we want to do is use this current like a switch to allow the motor to then get power from a better source. This is why we have the wonderful **transistor**!

Add an NPN transistor and setup your circuit like this. You won't need to edit any code.

This example is at ictsoeasy.co.uk/book2/#B2Ex16

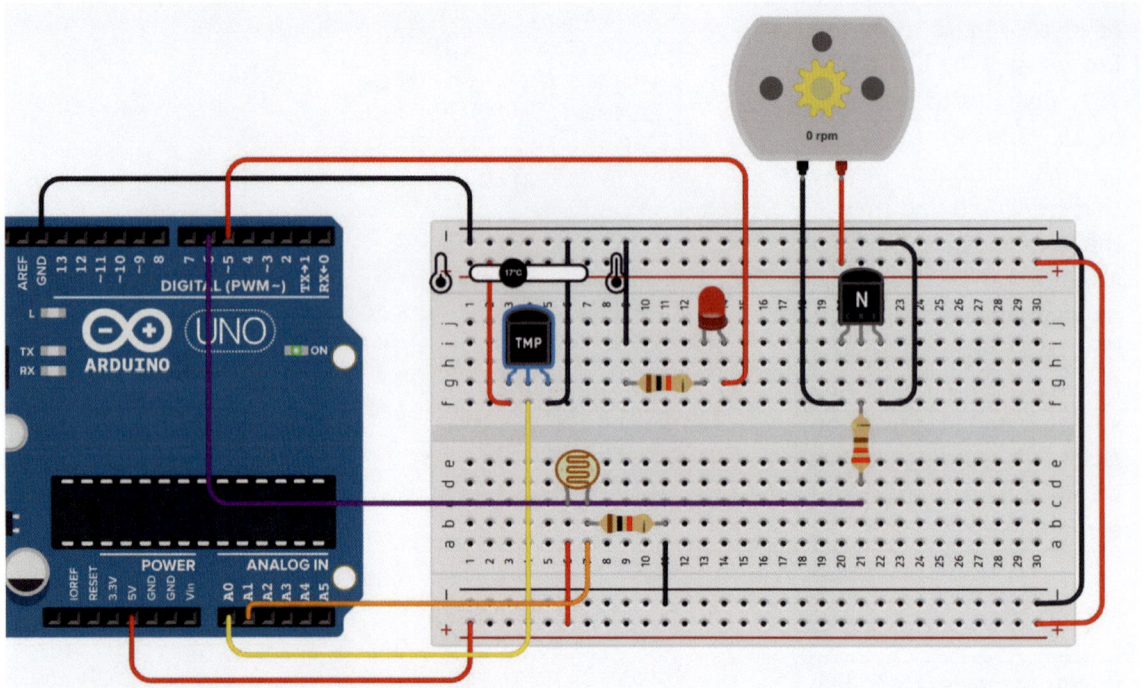

Using the transistor the current flows directly from the positive rail in to the motor, then tries to get to ground flowing into the C (collector) pin of the transistor. This is where it stops – it can't get any further! However, if we send a HIGH signal from pin 6 through the purple wire (and through that 220 ohm resistor (transistors really don't take much!) into the B (base) pin, then the transistor closes its internal switch, letting the motor power carry on to ground through the E (emitter) pin, and the motor will spin much faster!

The same method can be used to allow a motor to access 9v power or 3.3v power by having a separate positive feed for the motor (and both grounds being connected)

Challenges:

11. Our LED isn't very bright either, is it? Can you add another NPN transistor so it can use a separate feed?
12. Can you add a 9v battery for your motor to turn faster?

You can see our answers to the challenges here:

ictsoeasy.co.uk/book2/#B2Ch11
and…
ictsoeasy.co.uk/book2/#B2Ch12

Index

Using Physical Hardware

While using an emulator such as TinkerCad is great, and saves a lot of time getting computers and microcontrollers to talk to one another, it is always more fun having a go with real equipment. The list below is a list of all of the components you will need to engage with the projects in this book. You can source them from various suppliers or if you prefer follow the link at the bottom to buy them directly from ICT So Easy.

- Arduino MicroController – most will do but we like the MKR Wifi 1010 as a good mix of power, cost and connectivity.
- Breadboard for prototyping .
- LEDs (any colour will do!) - we used seven.
- Pushbutton switches – we used 2.
- Resistors – we use 7x220 Ohm and 1x10 kOhm.
- Potentiometer – we used a 3-pin 10kOhm.
- Photoresistor – we used one.
- Temperature sensor – we used one.
- DC Motor – we used one.
- NPN Transistor – we used two.
- Male to male jumper wires for connecting components to the jumper bord – a selection of sizes is good.

Kits, when available can be purchased from https://ictsoeasy.co.uk/book2/#B2Hardware

Printed in Great Britain
by Amazon